Contents

How's your balance?

When it comes to keeping your body fit and well and helping it to grow, eating a healthy and balanced diet is super important. A balanced diet means eating the right amount of different foods, but how do we know what is the right amount?

Why is balance important?

We all know that some foods are better for you than others. Foods such as fruit and vegetables contain more vitamins and minerals than foods like sweets and cakes. However, we need the fats and sugars that are in sweets and cakes to keep our bodies healthy, too – just not as much of them! For this reason, it's important to pick a wide variety of foods and to keep the right balance between the amount of healthy food you eat, and the less healthy items.

The fab five

All foods can be put into one of five groups:

- Bread, other cereals and potatoes
- Meat, fish and alternatives
- Fruit and vegetables
- Milk and dairy foods
- Foods that contain fats and sugars

The right balance

This plate shows how much of the food you eat should come from each group. One-third of the plate is filled with fruit and vegetables, one-third is filled with food from the bread, other cereals and potatoes group, and the last third is made up of the meat, fish and alternatives group, the fats and sugars group and the dairy group. Get this right, and you're perfectly balanced!

Weblink

Some countries, such as the USA and Australia, use a special food pyramid to help explain how to eat a healthy and balanced diet. To find out more, visit www.mypyramid.gov/kids

fruit and vegetables
(for example apples, broccoli, green beans and fruit juice)

bread, other cereals and potatoes
(such as bread, breakfast cereals and pasta)

milk and dairy foods
(includes things like milk, cheese and yoghurt)

meat, fish and alternatives
(such as pork, beef, chicken, tuna and tofu)

foods that contain fats and sugars
(for example, butter, mayonnaise, sweets and jam)

Just like plants!

Plants need water and sunshine to grow healthy and strong, and so do children! So, as well as eating a balanced diet, drink plenty of fluids, such as water and fruit juice, and get some fresh air every day – even if it's cold and rainy!

Fabulous fruit

This book is all about fruit from the fruit and vegetables group. Fruit is full of **vitamins**, **minerals** and **fibre**, which help to keep you healthy on both the inside and the outside. It grows in all shapes, sizes and colours and is one of the best foods for you to eat.

Science bit

Fruit contains lots of the important vitamins and minerals that our bodies need to stay fit and healthy. Vitamin A is good for our eyesight and helps our skin stay clear and in good condition. It can be found in apricots, nectarines and cantaloupe melons. B vitamins, found in **citrus fruits** such as oranges and satsumas, help give us energy. Vitamin C, also found in citrus fruits, helps us to fight colds and other illnesses. So, eat a variety of fruit to keep you bright and lively, fit for school and home!

Quick tip

Always wash fruit that does not need **peeling** by holding it under a running cold-water tap for a few seconds. Do this at home, before the fruit goes into your lunchbox.

Coconut

Pomegranate

Avocado

Orange

Tomato

Kiwi fruit

Blackberries

Get fit with fibre

Many fruits have **peel** and this is where lots of magic fibre can be found. Fibre makes sure we go to the toilet regularly and helps us to feel fit and raring to go. So, if the peel on your fruit is **edible**, such as apple and pear skins, make sure you eat it. Just don't try to eat banana skins or orange peel!

Fruit or veg?

Tomatoes, avocados and olives are all types of fruit, even though we tend to think of them as vegetables. They are fruits because they contain seeds or stones, so don't be surprised to see them in this book!

Bananas

Pear

Grapes

Apple

Peaches

Figs

Raspberries

Cherries

Strawberries

Lunch choice

Fruit salad

A fruit salad is a great way to get a tasty variety of fruit and is ideal for a packed lunch. Just chop up your favourite fruits and mix them together with some fruit juice.

Fruit juice

Sandwiches

Do it yourself

You can buy ready-made fruit salads, but it's easy and fun to make your own. If you don't have time in the morning, you can prepare the fruit the night before. Just pop it in the fridge overnight to keep it fresh.

Bite size

If you are slicing or **dicing** fruit to take to school, squeeze a little lemon juice over it to stop it turning brown. (It still tastes the same when it's brown, it just doesn't look as nice!)

Top tip

To stop your fruit from going soggy, put it in a tub without any juice. Add a little fresh fruit juice from a carton when you are ready to eat your fruit salad.

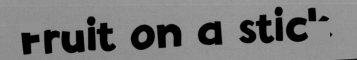
For a really unusual fruit snack, put together a fruit kebab. Cut pieces of fruit into bite-size chunks and thread them onto a small kebab stick. Squeeze with lemon juice and wrap in clear film or silver foil. Choose from pineapple chunks, satsuma segments, grapes, melon cubes and strawberry pieces.

Fruit salad

Watermelon is refreshing and cooling

CHECK IT OUT!

Try a fruit salad or a fruit kebab using three different types of melon:

Honeydew has a sweeter taste

Cantaloupe has a thicker texture

Five for five

Food experts recommend eating at least five **portions** of fruit and vegetables a day to help keep you healthy. Here are some ideas to make sure you get your five portions and still have time for some fun!

Good start

Have a glass of 100 per cent fruit juice in the morning, mixed with a little water. This counts as one portion, so only four more to go! Still have time before school? Why not have a delicious bowl of porridge mixed with a handful of berries or topped with banana slices and some runny honey?

Be a smoothie operator

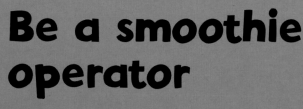

Why not make some super-cool smoothies? Ask an adult to blend three or four pieces of your favourite fruit with half a banana. You may need to add a little fruit juice if your smoothie is too thick. Pour into a flask and sip throughout the day. Fantastic!

Easy as A, B, C

Choose three pieces of fruit to eat throughout the day – one for your morning break, one to eat at lunchtime and one for an afternoon snack. Eat the fruit in alphabetical order – apple, banana, satsuma! Have some vegetables at lunchtime and some more with your evening meal and you've done it – you've had your five portions.

In disguise

Buy a plain yoghurt and pour it into a container. Mix in a load of your favourite fruit and enjoy as a lunchbox pudding. Alternatively, add chopped fruit to a tub of rice pudding or, for a special treat, chocolate mousse.

Fondue fun

Organize a **fondue** with your friends. Ask each person to bring a tub of fruit, cut into chunks. You will also need a fork each and a large bowl or tub of yoghurt. Spread out the tubs of fruit and pour the yoghurt into a bowl. Spear a piece of fruit onto a fork, dip into the yoghurt and eat.

Weblink

Find out more about why eating five portions of fruit and veg a day is so good for you at www.5aday.nhs.uk. There are great recipes to try out and some fun games to play, too.

Dried fruit

When is a grape not a grape? When it's a raisin!
Raisins, currants and sultanas are all dried grapes.

From vine to super snack

This is what the grapes look like before they are picked. They grow on a **vine**.

When the grapes are ripe, they are handpicked and laid out on paper sheets to dry naturally in the sun.

The dried grapes are then put on a truck and taken to a factory where they are inspected and selected for packaging.

Finally, the boxes of raisins are delivered to shops and supermarkets.

Bite size

Half a kilo of grapes makes only a handful of raisins.

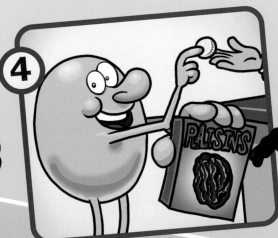

What's a prune?

Well, it's not a giant grape! In fact, a prune is a dried plum. Prunes are a great source of fibre and can be eaten hot or cold, by themselves or in a fruit salad.

What else is dried out?

Today, loads of fruit is available dried. Here's just a small selection:

Supersnack

Dried fruit is easy to nibble when mid-morning or afternoon hunger pangs strike. It lasts for ages and ages before it goes off, it's tasty and it's easy to pop in your lunchbox.

And guess what? It counts as one of your recommended portions of fruit and veg, too. Dried fruit? A lunchbox winner!

Apricots

Banana chips

Figs

Cherries

Mango slices

Lunch choice

Pasta salad with fruit

Fruit is such a versatile food that you can easily mix it in with a **savoury** salad for a fruity lunch that tastes as good as it looks.

Mix it!

Most fruits can be mixed with rice and pasta to make a tasty main course. Try pomegranate seeds, green grapes and raisins with brown pasta salad, or add some chopped satsumas and pineapple to a rice salad. For a pretty, pink lunch, mix diced beetroot with pasta and chopped apple.

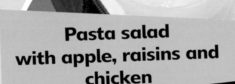

Apple

Rice pudding

Fruit juice

Pasta salad with apple, raisins and chicken

Pomegranate, green grapes and raisins

Apples and pears

For a light summer salad, try a mix of fresh green salad leaves with chopped apples and pears tossed in a little lemon juice. Sprinkle some cheese shavings over the top. Keep all the ingredients in different bags and tubs, and mix together when you are ready to eat.

Easy does it

For an easy lunchbox meal, try a chunk of cheese with a brown roll and an apple, or a cheese sandwich with an apple. Cottage cheese is also great for mixing with fruit – try chopped apples, satsumas and pineapple and eat straight from the tub or as a filling for a roll or a bagel.

Peach

All of these fruits taste great when eaten as part of a savoury snack. Try them and see...

Avocado

Mango

Nectarines

Tomatoes

Apricots

Strawberries

Tropical fruits

Apples, pears and oranges are all fruits that we know well, but there are loads of other fruits on sale that come from all around the world. Have you tried any of these?

Slice and scoop

Mangoes, papayas, passion fruit and guavas all originally came from hot places, such as the West Indies, South America and Asia. These fruits are bursting with vitamins and are great to eat by themselves or in a fruit salad. Some of these tropical fruits are full of juice and can get a bit sticky, so make sure you have some tissues or wipes for your fingers and chin!

Papaya

Mango

Guava

Passion fruit

Little gems

Pomegranates are difficult to eat at school, but you can prepare them the day before. Cut open a pomegranate and pop out the seeds into a small tub. You can then eat them at morning or afternoon break, like sweets.

Not what it seems

Although the kiwi fruit is grown mainly in New Zealand, it originally comes from China and is also known as a Chinese gooseberry. Each kiwi fruit contains nearly all the vitamin C you need for one day and is small enough to pop into any lunchbox. Slice it in half and scoop out the tasty flesh, pips and all, with a spoon.

Weblink

Fancy making a cool Caribbean fruit salad using all sorts of tasty tropical fruit? Visit www.food.gov.uk/healthiereating/nutritionschools/bus/recipes/146122 for a great recipe.

Pomegranates

Kiwi fruit

Lychees

Lookout for lychees

These small, round fruits also originally came from China. They are sold mostly in cans but they are sometimes on sale fresh. Pop a few fresh lychees into your lunchbox. Peel off the skin and eat the flesh, but be careful not to swallow the large brown pip in the centre.

Fruit juice

To keep healthy, what you drink is just as important as what you eat.

Fruity thirst buster

Some fruit drinks are much better for you than others. Lots of 'real' fruit juice drinks are sweetened with sugar. Look out for 100 per cent fruit juices, without anything added, and drink half juice, half water for a real thirst quencher.

Why do I need water?

Your body is made up mostly of water. A lot of this water is lost every day when you sweat and go to the toilet. To replace the water you lose, you need to drink at least one and a half to two litres of fluid every day. Drinking lots of water and juice keeps your skin clear and helps you to concentrate when you're doing those tricky maths problems.

Bite Size

Fruit juice made from **concentrate** has water added. 100 per cent fruit juice does not, so it has more vitamins.

On tap

The taste of your tap water depends on where you live. If you like the taste, tap water is the best drink for you, so get gulping! If you don't like the taste, you can always ask a grown-up to buy a filter jug. Keep it topped up in the fridge and use it to fill an empty bottle to take to school.

CHECK IT OUT!

Like fruit juice, some fruit squashes and **cordials** are loaded with extra sugar. Check the label to see just what you're getting.

Try it!

Fizzy, fruit-flavoured drinks are often full of sugar, so don't drink too much and remember to drink water and fresh fruit juice, too.

Super starter

For a healthy start to the day, or a tasty treat to take to school, try making your own fruit drinks at home. Blend together a fruit smoothie or squeeze some oranges for a vitamin burst that will get you off to a great start. It might even get you through a heavy science lesson!

1 Cut three medium-size oranges in half (ask an adult to help!).

2 Squeeze the oranges. Twisting a fork into each orange half will help you to extract all the juice.

3 Remove any pips, pour into a glass and... enjoy. Simple!

Canned and frozen

Most fresh fruit is only available at certain times of the year, but frozen or canned fruit means you can enjoy your favourites at any time.

Seasonal showdown

Most fruits grow at certain times of the year. These are called **seasonal** fruits and are on sale in shops and supermarkets for a short time each year. Strawberries, for example, are available during the summer season. However, most fruits can now be canned or frozen, so are available all year round.

CHECK IT OUT!

Canned fruit is just as good for you as fresh fruit. However, try not to buy canned fruit in syrup, as this is full of sugar. Check out the label and go for natural juices – just as tasty!

Bite size

Buying a can of fruit is a great way to try new fruits, especially if you're not sure how to peel or eat the fresh fruit. The canned fruit is already prepared for you, so there's no excuse not to try something new!

'Can' you guess?

Which fruits do you think are in the four cans below?
(Answers at the bottom of the page.)

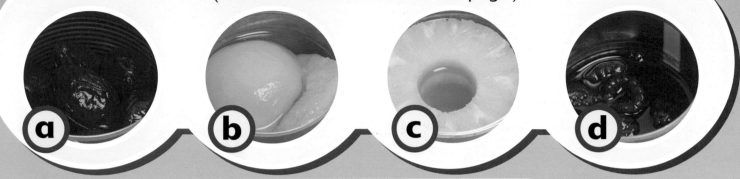

a   b   c   d

Get uncanned

It's so easy to make tasty lunchbox puddings with canned fruit.

1 Open some cans of your favourite fruits such as pineapple, pears and **mandarins**.

2 Mix the fruit together in a large bowl.

3 Put a couple of large tablespoonfuls into a tub, ready to take to school. You can keep the rest in the fridge and enjoy a scrumptious, fruity treat every day of the gweek. Easy, peasy, pudding!

Chill out!

On a hot day, chill out with this super fruit salad. Put some mixed frozen fruit in a tub in the morning – try a berry mix with blackberries, raspberries and strawberries. By lunchtime, the fruit will have thawed enough for you to eat, but will still be nice and cool and packed with loads of vitamins. Great for picnics, barbecues or school packed lunches!

An apple a day

'An apple a day keeps the doctor away' is an old saying. Apples are a good source of fibre, vitamins and minerals. Remember, for maximum goodness, keep the skin on.

Apple attack

There are over 2000 different varieties of apples grown around the world. Only a small number of these ever reach the supermarket or shops, which is just as well or you wouldn't be able to move for shelves full of apples!

Bite size

Don't worry if you swallow the odd apple pip – an apple tree won't grow in your tummy!

Apple rations

There are loads of ways to get your apple ration.
Why not try making apple purée? Simply peel an apple or two and pop them in a blender with a little milk or yoghurt. Blend until the apples become a smooth, thick mixture. You can then pour your purée over ice cream, mix it with rice pudding, spoon it over natural yoghurt or just enjoy it as it is, with a big dollop of jam or honey. Delicious! Alternatively, why not try a glass of apple juice (no added sugar!), mixed with water.

Pink Lady – pinkish-green, sweet and tangy.

Fruit stall

Here is a selection of just some of the apples you might see in shops. Why not try a different apple every day and see which is your favourite?

Braeburn – red and yellow, sweet and juicy.

Granny Smith – green, crisp and firm.

Empire – dark red, crunchy and tangy.

Golden Delicious – light green and crisp.

Fuji – reddish-pink, crisp and sweet.

Pinboard

Check out how fruit is eaten in other countries...

The Caribbean

In the Caribbean, fresh fruit such as this watermelon is eaten every day.

Australia

Pavlova is a meringue base filled with cream and fresh fruit, usually strawberries. It was created in Australia and is named after a ballerina called Anna Pavlova.

Italy

In Italy, people keep cool with water ices or sorbets made from fresh fruit juice such as orange or lemon juice.

Sweden

In many countries, such as Sweden, Norway and Poland, they make cold fruit soups.

Switzerland

In Switzerland, they dip pieces of fruit into melted-chocolate fondue.

Jamaica

Ackee is the national fruit of Jamaica and is eaten with fish dishes.

Quiz time

Multiple-choice

1. Which of the following is NOT a fruit?

a. grapes

b. olives

c. peaches

d. broccoli

2. Which vitamins are found in fruit?

a. vitamin A

b. vitamin B

c. vitamin C

d. all of the above

3. Which of these tastes good with most fruit?

a. mustard

b. yoghurt

c. low-fat mayo

d. tomato ketchup

4. Which of the following ways can you eat fruit?

a. in a smoothie

b. fresh!

c. as a fruit fondue

d. juiced

e. all of the above

5. Which of the following are types of melon?

a. honeydew

b. cantaloupe

c. passion fruit

d. kiwi

Match the fruit with its colour

Yellow

Mango

White

Green

Strawberries

Banana

Coconut

Red

Orange

Kiwi

True or false?

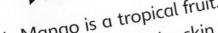

1. Mango is a tropical fruit.
2. You should eat the skin of lychees.
3. There are more than two million types of apples.
4. Ackee is a type of fruit from Jamaica.
5. Canned fruit is high in sugar.
6. Cantaloupe is a type of berry.
7. Fibre is good for you.
8. Apples have no seeds.
9. All fruit juice contains the same amount of sugar.
10. All fruit is low in fat.

What's the answer?

1. Which type of fruit provides the most vitamins and minerals?
2. Why is it important to eat a variety of fruits?
3. Can you name a fruit for every colour in the rainbow?
4. Which is healthier: fresh, canned or dried fruit? Why?
5. Plan a lunchbox menu for a week so that every day includes a different fruit eaten in a different way.

Answers

What's the answer?
There is not necessarily a right or a wrong answer to these questions, so discuss your answers with your teacher or a parent.

True or false?
1. TRUE
2. FALSE
3. FALSE
4. TRUE
5. FALSE
6. FALSE
7. TRUE
8. FALSE
9. FALSE
10. TRUE

Match the fruit with its colour
Strawberries – red
Mango – orange
Kiwi – green
Coconut – white
Banana – yellow

Multiple-choice
1. d – broccoli
2. d – all of the above
3. b – yoghurt
4. e – all of the above
5. a and b – honeydew and cantaloupe

Glossary

citrus fruits Juicy, acidic fruits such as oranges, grapefruit, limes and lemons

concentrate When a substance is reduced down to make it stronger. Fruit juice made from concentrate has lots of water added to the concentrate mixture to dilute it

cordial A fruit syrup that you dilute with water to make a drink

dicing Chopping into small pieces

edible Food that is fresh and tasty and which can be eaten without making you ill

fibre The part of your food that helps your digestion work properly and makes sure you go to the toilet regularly

fondue A special way of eating meat, vegetables or fruit chunks by using a long fork to dip them into hot oil, melted cheese or melted chocolate

mandarin A small citrus fruit, a little like an orange

minerals Substances found in certain foods which help to keep our bodies healthy, for example calcium, which helps strengthen bones and teeth

peel (verb) Removing the skin from a piece of fruit

peel (noun) The outside layer of a piece of fruit such as an orange, banana or apple

portion The amount of one type of food or drink that we eat at one meal

savoury Food that is not sweet

seasonal Food that grows at certain times of the year, for example, strawberries grow during the summer season

vine The plant that grapes grow on

vitamins Substances found in the food we eat that are essential for us to stay healthy. There are many different vitamins, such as A, B, C and D

Index

Parents' and teachers' notes

• Have a general talk about fruit. How much do the children know about fruit? Do they eat much fruit? If so, which fruits do they eat?

• Do the children have fruit at school? Do they bring in their own fruit or eat fruit provided at school?

• Do the children prefer fruit raw or cooked? Can they name some cooked fruit puddings such as fruit pies or crumble? Does the same fruit taste different depending on whether it is cooked or eaten raw?

• Go through the book looking at the pictures of the fruit. Do the children recognize the different fruits? Have they eaten them? If not, would they like to?

• Build a fruit salad picture. Cut out pictures of fruit from magazines and make a huge fruit montage.

• If you can, organize a fruit tasting. Ask the children to bring in different types of fruit. Before you cut the fruit, ask the children to smell it and say if they like the smell or not. Cut the fruit into chunks. Blindfold the children and ask them to try the fruit. What do they think it is? (For any tastings, ask each child to bring in a letter from their parents or guardians granting permission.)

• Discuss the difference between sweet, sour and bitter. Are some fruits sweeter than others? Are some fruits bitter or sour?

• Talk about fruit textures. Buy a selection of fruit such as apricots, pineapple, kiwi fruit, oranges and apples. Discuss how the different fruits feel. What words would the children use to describe them?

• Write a poem about fruit. Use words such as 'sweet', 'crunchy', 'juicy', 'sour', 'soft' and 'squidgy'.